End Anxiety & Stop Worrying In 10 Minutes

A Stepwise Guide To Start Living Your Best Life With Courage & Confidence

GREGG GRAY

End Anxiety & Stop Worrying In 10 Minutes: A Stepwise Guide To Start Living Your Best Life With Courage & Confidence

Copyright © 2019 Gregg Gray

ISBN: 9781075804298

All rights reserved. No part of this guide may be reproduced in any form without permission in writing from the publisher except in the case of brief quotations embodied in critical articles or reviews.

Legal & Disclaimer

The information contained in this book and its contents is not designed to replace or take the place of any form of medical or professional advice; and is not meant to replace the need for independent medical, financial, legal or other professional advice or services, as may be required. The content and information in this book have been provided for educational and entertainment purposes only.

The content and information contained in this book have been compiled from sources deemed reliable, and it is accurate to the best of the Author's knowledge, information, and belief. However, the Author cannot guarantee its accuracy and validity and cannot be held liable for any errors and/or omissions. Further, changes are periodically made to this book as and when needed. Where appropriate and/or necessary, you must consult a professional (including but not limited to your doctor, attorney, financial advisor or such other professional advisor) before using any of the suggested remedies, techniques, or information in this book.

Upon using the contents and information contained in this book, you agree to hold harmless the Author from and against any damages, costs, and expenses, including any legal fees potentially resulting from the application of any of the information provided by this book. This disclaimer applies to any loss, damages or injury caused by the use and application, whether directly or indirectly, of any advice or information presented, whether for breach of contract, tort, negligence, personal injury, criminal intent, or under any other cause of action.

You agree to accept all risks of using the information presented inside this book. You agree that by continuing to read this book, where appropriate and/or necessary, you shall consult a professional (including but not limited to your doctor, attorney, or financial advisor or such other advisor as needed) before using any of the suggested remedies, techniques, or information in this book.

CONTENTS

1. **INTRODUCTION** — 1
2. **CHAPTER ONE**: — 3
   KNOWING YOUR ENEMIES WELL IS HALF THE BATTLE
3. **CHAPTER TWO**: — 7
   THE SECRET WORKINGS OF YOUR ENEMIES
4. **CHAPTER THREE**: — 13
   GOOD HABITS & PRACTICES TO INCULCATE TOWARDS A WORRY-FREE LIFE
5. **CHAPTER FOUR**: — 19
   THE SIX PROVEN 10-MINUTE QUICK REMEDIES
6. **CHAPTER FIVE**: — 25
   PRACTICAL 10-MINUTE FUN ACTIVITIES TO KEEP IT TOGETHER
7. **CONCLUSION** — 29

INTRODUCTION

Anxiety is not always bad, but when it persists, it becomes necessary to look for an effective solution. Nobody can boldly tell you that they haven't ever felt anxious about something in their lives. Feeling anxious occasionally is perfectly normal, but when the feeling exceeds a manageable level, doctors may call it anxiety disorder. When it gets to this point, the search for medication starts.

Worry, on the other hand, is not a new word. We've gotten so familiar with saying "don't worry" that right now; everybody seems to be worried about something all the time. Indeed, all of us may have at one point been worried about a task, an exam, a project, or others. However, the thing to note is that persistent worry may lead to anxiety.

Many times, issues and challenges of life can lead us to worry, whether we like it or not. Worry has become a part of our lives. But the question is, will you allow it to take over your life? Are you willing to subject your mind and body to a series of doctor's diagnosis and incessant medications? We hope not.

The truth is, we have the healthy kinds of anxiety. There are times when being anxious can alert you of danger and invariably save your life. Well, that's not the type we are concerned about here. Our focus is on the level where you can't eat, rest, sleep, or relax due to constant worrying. We are talking about the stage where you've become anxious over the smallest and most insignificant issues. Where you've become popular for always being nervous, apprehensive, and jumpy.

This e-book aims to help you overcome anxiety and stop worrying through our tips and techniques that wouldn't take more than ten minutes of your time. This e-book will start by giving you an insight into anxiety and its consequences. You'll get to know how a constant feeling of worry and anxiousness may lead to anxiety disorders. We've also presented some important tips that can help you to live without the bonds of anxiety disorder. Simple activities that everyone can practice to overcome this condition are available here.

Are you always unsure of what to do when faced with a panic attack? Would you love to experience calm in ten minutes? We're going to introduce you to a whole new world of effective remedies for unexpected attacks. How would you love to be in charge of your life without allowing challenges to weigh you down? We have simple exercises that you can do in ten minutes to eliminate excessive worry. These remedies, exercises, and tips are all very exciting. Spare ten minutes of your time on them and start living your best life with courage and confidence.

CHAPTER ONE: KNOWING YOUR ENEMIES WELL IS HALF THE BATTLE

Anxiety

Google and reputable dictionaries tell us that anxiety is when someone feels worried, nervous, distressed or uneasy about what is happening now, an outcome or what may likely happen in the future due to fear of misfortune or imminent danger. When anxiety turns into an extreme condition and becomes a health concern, doctors call it anxiety disorder. Anxiety is a product of worry and fear. If you can overcome these two feelings, you'll have better chances of living without bonds.

Worry

Google has defined it as being anxious or worked up about an actual problem or a potential problem. When your mind seems not to rest over a particular thing, we say you are worried about it. Worrying excessively has never helped anybody. Instead, it makes us think, imagine, feel, and act irrationally due to a threat or feared consequences. Also, it doesn't lead to actual solutions but drags you into anxiety. Moreover, it can affect your life negatively by upturning your relationships, habits, and sleep. The most dangerous aspect is that some people who are known as worrywarts or nervous nellies have been seen relying on drugs, food, cigarette, and alcohol just to cope.

Anxiety Disorders

There are many types of anxiety disorders, but we will discuss five out of them all very briefly. This will enable you to understand what you are feeling right now or what someone close to you is battling every day.

1. Generalized Anxiety Disorder

This type is characterized by worry and excessive anxiousness. When someone worries about issues in everyday life, work-related issues, or health challenges for more than six months, there's cause for alarm. Whatever keeps an individual on edge, for a long time is GAD.

Some of the symptoms of a person suffering from generalized anxiety disorders are:
- Restlessness or being on edge
- Gets easily tired
- Irritations and outbursts over little things
- Muscle tension
- Blanking out during important tasks
- Not being able to sleep quickly or restfully
- Can't stop worrying

2. Panic Disorder

This is characterized by the attack of sudden intense fear when confronted with a situation or object that you are afraid of.

Panic attacks come with the following symptoms:
- Sweating
- Accelerated heart rates
- Pounding heartbeat
- Uncontrollable trembling

- Choking feelings, shortness of breath, and feelings of being out of control

This type of P.D is very uncomfortable because the victim may always worry about the next bout. In this state, there's no way to be productive or live freely.

3. Phobia

People usually tell us this, "I have a phobia for crawling things" or "I have a phobia for dogs." People with this type of disorder often have a specific situation or object that paralyzes them with fear. Sometimes, the object may not even be as harmful as they imagine or fear.

The symptoms:
- Irrational worry about an encounter with the object
- Trying hard to avoid the object at all costs
- Being suddenly anxious when they face the object
- Endure the object with anxiety
  Some common types of phobias include:
- Simple Phobia is fear for a specific situation or object such as heights, flying, blood, injections, some animals, etc.
- Agoraphobia is fear for specific activities such as using public transport, fear of enclosed or open spaces, staying outside your home alone, or being in crowded areas or standing in a queue.
- Social phobia is characterized by a fear of social situations or performance.

4. Separation Anxiety Disorder

The fear and worry about losing a person you are devoted to or close to is called separation anxiety disorder. This unhealthy anxiety can make such an individual cling to that person incessantly. Sometimes, he/she can even have nightmares of a separation

5. Selective Mutism

This condition is rare, but it exists. Have you ever seen someone stand on a stage and finds it hard to utter a word? The symptoms sometimes are extreme shyness, fear of embarrassment, temper tantrums, clinging behaviors, withdrawal, and compulsive traits.

CHAPTER TWO: THE SECRET WORKINGS OF YOUR ENEMIES

Researchers have not yet discovered the main causes of anxiety disorders. However, they have mentioned a few things that may likely be the reasons for it.

1. Brain Changes
Researchers have said that anxiety disorder is a mental illness, and as such, it can be triggered by the changes in the brain. According to them, if the part of the brain which controls fear or other emotions malfunction, it may lead to A.D. For instance, prolonged stress can affect the part of the brain that controls our moods. When it occurs, anxiety disorder becomes imminent.

2. Genes
Studies have also proved that A.D might be hereditary just like we inherit eye color, hair texture, etc. from our parents. Likewise, an anxiety disorder can also exist in a family line.

3. Traumas
Sometimes an event or trauma which we faced as a child or as an adult may lead to anxiety disorder. For instance, someone who was once bitten by a snake may panic whenever

he/she sees it.

Other common reasons why we develop anxiety disorders are:

4. Work Stress
When you have loads of work with short deadlines, you can't help but feel anxious about them. Sometimes, a task with limited sources for a solution can evoke fear. It happens to everyone, yes, but we shouldn't make it a habit.

5. Social Pressure
Many people who try hard to please their friends, colleagues, or group, will always feel anxious. It can cause an individual to change his/her values, attitude, or behavior to match that of the peers. You'll notice that you're always anxious and afraid of being different. Being unique doesn't hurt anyone, and instead of becoming something you're not, why not remain different.

6. Drug Use
It doesn't matter if you're a newbie or a drug addict. Once you've cultivated the habit of taking drugs, you'll always be anxious. A newbie will worry about being caught and how to face parents, friends, spouse, or colleagues. An addict, on the other hand, will be anxious about his next package. Sometimes, they may be restless and jumpy, thereby falling into anxiety.

7. Medical Worries
Health issues can make you anxious. It may be that you need money to buy drugs, or you're worried about the doctor's diagnosis. Also, when a child or spouse is sick, you may become very anxious. Whatever the reason, being anxious when you face a medical situation causes more harm than good.

8. Financial Challenges
This is one reason for being anxious. At one point in life,

your finances may not be adequate in answering your needs. When you think about everything you've got to do, you may become anxious unknowingly.

Why You Would Keep Your Enemies Closer (Too Close!)

People worry for different reasons. But, many of the bad things we spent time worrying about didn't happen. So why can't we stop? Why do we worry all the time even when we know that it's harmful? Let's consider some of the reasons:

1. Worry Brings Temporary Relief From Problems

When you worry about an issue, it always seems as if you'll find the solution. The truth is that you are just running away from the feeling of helplessness.

2. It Seems To Help Us Avoid Disappointment

Many people worry because they don't want to be taken unaware or surprised by a bad outcome. So, they worry and maybe prepare their minds for an imminent disappointment.

3. Worry Is Often Interpreted As Concern

Some people worry because they want people to see that they care. It's funny though because someone in a predicament doesn't need to worry. What they need is a solution. Worrying is not the show of concern but more like a stressor. So, if you care, get practical with a solution. It's better that way!

4. It Spurs Me Into Action

You may feel like when you worry; it motivates you to take action. However, the reverse is the case. Worry is unproductive. Some people seem to indulge in it as a way to motivate themselves. However, it only weakens your mind and stresses your body out.

5. Worry Brings Solutions To Problems

Well, that's not true. Worrying about a matter will not

bring solutions to it. We've come to realize that the more you worry, the bigger the problem seems. Sometimes, when you have a difficult task to execute, don't waste your time worrying that you'll not achieve it. Instead, start nicking at it gradually, and before you know, it's solved.

8 Signs
To Watch Out For Before It's Too Late

You can't wake up one morning and become a patient of anxiety disorder. It starts with worry and graduates to a health concern. So, let's look at some of the symptoms that you shouldn't ignore:

1. Chronic Worrying

If you continue to worry about something even with adequate reassurances, something is going wrong.

2. The Changes In Your Body Are Affecting You

Healthy anxiety will have some symptoms we agree with. However, when these symptoms don't go away easily or subside quickly, think about it seriously.

3. You Become Absent-Minded & Can't Concentrate

Other factors such as lack of sleep or depression can cause this too. However, anxiety can also cause you to lose focus and become unable to concentrate on one thing.

4. Sleeplessness

If you always find it hard to sleep due to fear and worry, night after night, it is time to back-pedal a bit and take action before it leads to anxiety disorder.

5. Increased Level Of Irritability And Negativity

Anybody can be irritable when they are stressed out. However, when you find yourself always mad and unable to be patient, look inwards, and take a break.

6. Problems Everywhere - School Or Work

You can't be motivated to put in your best if you're constantly anxious. So, when you start lagging in things you used to do well before, it's time to be careful.

7. Increased Relationship Issues
When your loved ones or friends no longer feel comfortable around you, you have to check your behavior. For instance, you are curt with people, always on edge or reluctant to engage in social activities. These are little signs that you're becoming over anxious.

8. Feeling Out-Of-Control
When you can't put your hands on how you're feeling or can't control your body reactions, there is a need to be concerned.

These signs are not suggesting that you have anxiety disorder already. They mean that you need to be concerned and see how you can stop them from spiraling out of control. Don't allow your habit of worrying to develop an anxiety disorder. Be careful, worry less, and live better.

The Top 4 Consequences For Indulging In Your Enemies

Anxiety may not kill, but it can lead to severe or life-threatening health challenges. These are some repercussions of untreated anxiety:

1. Depression
Anxiety and depression usually occur together. Someone suffering from anxiety disorder may gradually slip into depression. Therefore, don't ignore the signs. Instead, do something to be free. Depression can rob someone of life itself.

2. Substance Abuse
Anxiety disorder can lead to addiction. Someone with AD might turn to substances in a bid to calm his/her nerves. For instance, they can often depend on nicotine, alcohol, or other

drugs that provide a short-term feeling of calm. No matter what many people believe, all these substances can only offer relief that won't last.

3. Suicide

This is one of the results of untreated anxiety. The National Alliance on Mental Illness reveals that of all the people who committed suicide, 90% had one mental illness or the other. Also, the Substance Abuse & Mental Health Services Administration records that 4% of adults in the U.S have thought about committing suicide. As such, people who have social phobia or obsessive-compulsive disorder are at a higher risk for suicide. Now if the person also has depression, the risk goes higher.

4. Physical Sickness

Another reason to fight against anxiety is that it can lead to many illnesses. For instance, if you have chronic stress due to anxiety, it may lead to a weak immune system. The resultant effect is that your body will become a playground for bacterial diseases, flu, viral diseases, and colds.

CHAPTER THREE: GOOD HABITS & PRACTICES TO INCULCATE TOWARDS A WORRY-FREE LIFE

Anxiety and worry are habits, which many people developed over time. The search for solutions starts when the doctor says, "disorder." However, you can avoid these conditions if you prevent it in time. So, start with the tips available in this chapter.

5 Top Achievers' Approaches To Life

Worry leads to anxiety. If you can eliminate fear and worry in your life, you've won over anxiety. Don't waste your life worrying and miss the good things in life. Remember, the things we worry about don't always come to pass.

Emulate these simple habits and enjoy a worry-free life like top achievers.

1. Set Goals

People who live without worries set goals and focus on achieving them. By setting goals, you will have hope, vision, and direction. With these goals to guide your thoughts, plans, and steps, you can live without worry.

2. Focus On The Good

A worry-free individual thinks on the good sides of things, situations, people, and events. Don't feed your worry by focusing on your problems. Remember the good things and keep your mind there.

3. Take Action

Adopt the take-action nature of worry-free people. Don't put all the time into thinking, learning the steps, creating ideas but in the end, you don't implement them. Instead, decide on how to tackle a problem and act immediately.

Fear and worry can distract you. If you don't take action, you may worry about things that are not relevant to solving your challenges. And fear will set in. And the downward spiral begins.

4. Focus On Finding Solutions

Why worry about a problem when you can always look for a solution. Worry-free individuals refuse to be distracted. Instead, they focus on finding and creating solutions to their problems.

5. Take Risks

Top achievers take risks all the time. But before they do so, they need to build confidence by studying their options, weighing the odds, assessing the risks and contemplating the worst-case scenarios. Calculated risks. Calculations made, before taking risks, replace and eliminate fear and worry.

So, the next time you come against an elephant, remember to eat it with small bites. Break the challenge down into manageable steps. Make a list and tackle each step, one at a time. And finally, focus on the rewards that will likely come after taking the risk.

Face The Enemy & Overcome It

Every mile begins with a single step. You can stop worrying by changing some of your behavioral tendencies that feed it. One feeling associated with anxiety is fear. Being afraid of a situation, result, event that may not occur can stagnate your life. Therefore, instead of dwelling on uncertainties and hindering your success, start inculcating these twelve good practices and habits today.

1. Learn

Uncertainty leads to fear. When you equip yourself with enough information, your problems become lighter. If you understand it, you will know how to handle it and stop being afraid. So, when in doubt, don't waste your time sweating and fretting. Instead, do the following things:

    i.   Do some research or Google it
    ii.   Find the book and read it
    iii.   Consult with someone

2. Distract Your Mind

When you are stuck, STOP! Don't overthink. Find something else to do and change the focus of your mind. For instance, you can:

    i.   Hit the gym and do some serious workout
    ii.   Step out for a while and enjoy an exhilarating conversation with a friend
    iii.   Go for that visit you've been postponing

3. Face It

Don't avoid your fears. Charge towards it and watch it disappear.

    i.   If you're afraid of public places, start visiting such places
    ii.   Don't like animals? Go to the zoo sometimes or read about them
    iii.   Take public transport if you don't like strangers

It is always better to practice with someone the first time. You can join a group or ask a friend to help you. If you try and feel like bolting, tell your companion about it. Both of you can find ways to help you get through the experience.

4. Live In The Now

Are you always worrying and afraid of the future? It's good to think about the future but not all the time. If you can help it, live your life in the now and lessen your fears of tomorrow. Make a conscious effort and try out the following activities:

i. Notice the sound of the shower
ii. Watch the movement of rainfall
iii. Perceive the freshness of the morning
iv. Don't think about dinner in the morning.
v. Discover the different tastes of coffee
vi. Notice what other people are doing
vii. Listen to what your colleagues are saying
viii. Wait until Monday to tackle the job you have in the office.
ix. Participate in the things happening around you.
x. Bills, bills, and more bills. Don't allow these thoughts to make you anxious. Create a plan on how to pay them and follow it.

5. Postpone The Worry

Don't give it any time at all. Once worrying wants to interfere with your daily activities, stop it immediately. Remove them from your mind and note them down on your worry list for a designated worry time.

6. Discuss It

Talking to someone can help you to let go of worry. The right person can provide the insight you need to solve your problems. You can meet with your closest friends for simple issues. However, when the object of your worry grows beyond what they can handle, get professional advice.

7. Reduce Your Computer Habits

A computer screen can increase anxiety. Yes, that includes your handphones and tablets. If your social interactions center on the Internet, you may be spending more time than healthy watching the screens. Another thing to reduce is your social media time. Please, cut it down and eliminate unnecessary comparisons, regrets, and desires that make you anxious.

8. Exercise Is The Key

Decrease your worries faster by exercising your body. Exercise is good for the body, yes, but it also helps the mind to relax. You may be surprised that exercise works better than prescription drugs when it comes to reducing anxiety. You can dance, do Yoga or play tennis. Dancing lifts your spirit, yoga brings calm to your mind, and playing tennis takes your mind off your worries.

9. Meditate

Meditation helps to decrease worry. If you've not formed the habit yet, start it today and watch the difference it will make. There are many different schools of meditation. Do some research and find the nearest or most convenient meditation centers or schools and sign yourself up for a short course!

10. Aromatherapy Helps

Studies have shown that scents can alleviate worry and stress. Once you perceive the scent of some essential oils, it helps you to feel lighter. For instance, researchers have discovered that grapefruit scent can reduce worry so, try it out next time and feel better.

11. Change Your Way Of Thinking

Life can't be perfect, so accept it and ignore the reasons for worrying unnecessarily. Also, life is very unpredictable. If you start feeling low that your plans didn't work, anxiety will creep in. Therefore, change those unhealthy thought patterns.

12. Eat Healthily

Eat to maintain a functional body system. Lean on energy giving foods. Anxiety can leave you weak. Therefore, eat when the body needs it. Stock your kitchen with all your favorite foods at all times. If you can't cook sometimes, eat out or have them deliver it to you. You need your blood sugar to be normal, and your body system functional at all times.

Don't spend time worrying about a problem or situation when you can spend lesser time solving it. So, if you must overcome anxiety, start now to overcome fear and worry.

CHAPTER FOUR: THE SIX PROVEN 10-MINUTE QUICK REMEDIES

Many situations can trigger panic attacks. Learn to catch yourself and see it coming. Please refer to *Chapter One: Knowing Your Enemies Well Is Half The Battle*, under *Panic Disorder*, to find the list of common body reactions or symptoms that foreshadow a panic attack. Consequently, try out these six proven 10-minute quick remedies and feel better in a blink.

1. Breathing

Have you ever leveraged the power of breathing for calm? Many people will tell you that when they don't want to act in anger, they breathe for some minutes. Try out these breathing techniques the next time you panic.

Belly Breathing
- Sit on a comfortable chair
- Close your eyes
- Focus on your breathing
- Breathe through your nose
- Be as natural as you can, don't control it
- Feel how the air goes in and out through your nostrils

- Place a hand on the chest and the other hand below the ribcage
- Breathe in deeply for a count of four
- Hold it until you count three
- Contract the muscles of your abdomen
- Exhale through the mouth for a count of four

Continue until your mind focuses on the breathing sensation. Anytime your mind wanders, refocus it to the breaths.

Nose Breathing
- Sit comfortably and cross your legs
- Place your left hand on your left knee
- Breathe in and exhale
- Close the right nostril with your right thumb
- Inhale through the left nostril
- Pause for one second
- Close the left nostril using the ring finger
- Release the right nostril and exhale through it
- Inhale through the right nostril
- Pause for one second
- Close the right nostril again using the right thumb
- Release the left nostril and exhale through it

Go on with this alternate breathing two or three times. Afterward, sit quietly for some minutes before standing up.

5:20:10

You can prevent a sudden panic attack by taking power breaths. Let's practice.
- Breathe in for 5 seconds
- Hold your breath for 20 seconds
- Breathe out for 10 seconds

Do this as many times as it takes to stop the panic. If you complete a set and still feel that it's not enough, go for another round.

Buteyko Breathing

This breathing technique helps prevent hyperventilation

when you are getting anxious. That rapid breathing that feels like you're not getting enough oxygen and you're struggling to get enough air into the lungs. However, the cause is really an excessive inflow of oxygen. This Buteyko method will help you to recreate the balance.

Here's what you need to do:
- Sit on a comfortable chair
- Breathe in and out
- Once you've breathed out, use your fingers and pinch your nose
- Then hold your breath
- Hold it as long as you can and breathe out once you feel the urge
- Breathe in and out as usual
- After 30 to 60 seconds, repeat the process until you're relaxed and calm

We've shared some breathing remedies that can calm the rising tide of anxiety. If you're someone who always panics at every little thing, these remedies will help you. As soon as you remember them, it will take only a few minutes to calm down. Don't be shy of doing it anywhere. Everybody breathes. So nobody might even notice you doing your secret breathing techniques!

2. Progressive Muscle Relaxation

This is one quick remedy that would help your brain and muscles to relax. Anxiety causes our muscles to tense up. When it happens, the brain would automatically understand it as a sign of trouble. However, with PMR, you can stop it.

Here's what you will do:
- Sit down comfortably
- Start flexing your muscles as you count to ten
- Do this in groups and move from one muscle group to the next
- Flex each group for ten seconds and release the muscles for another ten seconds

- Feel the tension ebb away from your muscles and your brain

By relaxing your muscles, your mind will gradually calm down.

3. Visiting A Quiet Haven

We all know that the beach or a cabin in the woods can be very tranquil and calming. But how will you get there to calm down in ten minutes? Time to exercise your imagination! It gets easier the more you do it. Practice makes perfect.

- Close your eyes
- Block out all stimulus and focus on your breathing
- Take your mind to the cabin in the woods or the beach
- Focus on your surroundings
- Dig your toes into the beach sand
- How does it feel? Warm or cold
- If you are in the cabin, smell the scent of pine trees
- It is pleasant, isn't it?
- Feel the chilly air on your body

This "visit" will take your mind off whatever it was that triggered the panic and calm you down. Sound effect or ambiance soundtracks of the beach, waves or in the woods could be great accompaniments for getting you in the "zone". They are readily available on YouTube. Try plugging into one of them on your handphone before you begin your "sojourns".

4. Ground Yourself

This is a method of doing a tangible thing when anxiety strikes. There are many ways to achieve this.

Key Trace

- Pick up your key (house, car, etc)
- Drop it on your left palm
- Run one finger over it for 10 seconds

- Use another finger and trace the key for another 10 seconds
- Do the same with each finger on your right hand
- Always keep your eyes on the movement of your finger over the key

Ice Cube Grip
- Bring out an ice cube
- Hold it in one hand for ten seconds
- Drop it in the other hand and hold it for another ten seconds
- Do this until your mind calms down

This exercise can shift your mind from catastrophic thoughts to the cold in your palms. Before five minutes, you will experience more calm than you thought possible.

5. The Focus Trick

This is like a magic wand to stopping a panic attack. And it's great fun! Try it.
- Find an object and watch it closely
- Don't notice anything else beside it
- What patterns does it have?
- Try to describe them to yourself quietly
- What colors do you see?
- What is the shape, size, texture, temperature, and weight of the object?
- Focus your energy and notice everything about it
- Now, close your eyes and try to "see" the object in your mind's eye
- How many details can you still "see" on the object?

As you do this, your panic will subside gradually.

6. The Water Effect

Dehydration affects the mind negatively. With this remedy, you can bring calm to your nervous system.
- Fill a tall glass with cold water

- Close your eyes and start
- Sip gradually for 3 seconds
- Swallow it 3 times
- Pause for 2 seconds
- Sip for 2 seconds
- Swallow it 2 times and pause for 3 seconds
- Sip again for 1 second and swallow it in 1 gulp
- Pause for 4 seconds before starting again from the beginning
- Feel the coldness as it travels down your throat each time you swallow the cold water

This quick remedy never fails to calm nerves in the worst wreck. Plain water always works better than flavored drinks because its "neutral" taste has the effect of "resetting" the moods. Water at room temperature will work too if it is preferred over cold water.

CHAPTER FIVE: PRACTICAL 10-MINUTE FUN ACTIVITIES TO KEEP IT TOGETHER

These four simple activities can help you to understand and eliminate your fears and worries.

1. Pen It Down

- Pick a plain piece of paper
- Draw 2 vertical lines to divide the paper into 3 columns
- The title should be, "One thing I'm anxious about/putting off/see as risky
- In the column on the left, list everything you feel could go wrong if you're facing the worst case scenario
- In the center column, list the actions you could take to prevent the items in the worst case scenarios
- In the right column, list what your actions would be to solve the worst case scenario items if they come to pass

This exercise will help you to realize that the worst case scenarios you envisage may not occur. However, if they happen, you can still manage them without dying.

2. Color it Away

Do you remember how you used to concentrate on your coloring homework as a child? It's time to relive the feeling again. This time you are doing it to prevent excessive worrying. Do the following:
- Bring out a scrapbook
- Find a box of colored pencils
- Fill a page of your scrapbook with lines, circles, squares, or whatever shapes you like
- Overlap these shapes however you please
- Don't think or design, just draw
- When you're done filling the page start coloring the areas that are demarcated by the lines. These areas are probably the intersections of a few shapes that you've drawn
- Use whatever color you want, as many colors as you want. See if you could make sure that no adjacent areas have the same color
- Have crazy fun with it

This exercise might seem like a child's play but if you concentrate on it, you'll forget your worries before ten minutes.

3. Stick It Out

Many teenagers do this often. Sometimes, when you feel like anxiety is trying to steal your happiness, push it away by doing this exercise.
- Start a scrapbook
- Use any printouts you could get your hands on
- They could be magazines, handouts, pamphlets, bills, newspapers, etc.
- Cut out pictures of any object or people
- Paste these cutouts in the pages of your scrapbook in whichever way you like

- You can collage them together to tell a story
- Categorize them according to your own rules, or just be crazy
- Keep a collection of cutouts for your next epic montage!

4. Continue Without Limits

Exposure is the gradual and repetitive actions you must take to face your fears. It takes you closer to your fears until you're no longer anxious about them. Fear of exposure can stop you from achieving the best results, even after knowing what to do. You have to start, or else, you're not going to overcome anxiety.

So, if you're ready to start now, take these simple steps:

Step One: List What You Fear

The list should include all those things, places, or situations you fear. For instance, many people are afraid of: public speaking, meeting people, talking to strangers, trying new things, insects, animals, etc. Other things people fear include driving, needles, crowded places, animals, germs, etc.

Now, make a list of everything you fear.

Step Two: Rank The List

Start arranging them according to the extent you fear them. For instance, place the scariest at number one and continue like that until you come down to the least feared. You can even use a scale of zero to ten to rank them.

Step Three: Face The Fears

After completing step two above, the next thing is to practice. You can select any fear on the list and work on it. Don't expect a miracle. It's okay to be anxious as you face the fear. Don't be in a rush. Take your time to plan it and celebrate when you do it and succeed.

Step Four: Practice

This is not a one-off attempt. You need to practice every

day or once in a while. Constant practice will ensure faster results. Therefore, keep going until you overcome your fear. If you relax, you might forget the victory and relive the fear again.

Step Five: Reward
Facing your fears can't be easy at all. If you managed to conquer the object for even the littlest minutes, celebrate a little. Do you know why? You are a hero.

Fear can't dictate the pace of your life when you have all it takes to overcome it. Since we know that we are anxious about what we fear, face it, and eliminate anxiety from your life now.

CONCLUSION

We've come to the final parts of this e-book. Are you excited to start the journey to reclaiming your life? It's not easy, but you can do it if you prepare your mind. Don't allow the things you can defeat to dictate the direction of your life. Many times, we allow uncertainty and fear of the unknown to cripple us. Three things we've seen so far that can keep you restless and unhappy are fear, worry, and anxiety. Each of these enemies is somehow a part of human existence. However, it doesn't mean that they're okay. If you allow any of them or all to live with you, you've decided to say Godspeed to joy, peace, and freedom.

Anxiety is deadly. It may not kill directly, but it can lead to life-threatening conditions. You've seen some of the implications of allowing it to grow and fester. It starts with innocent worrying over something and gradually metamorphoses into an anxiety disorder. Would you be comfortable with being called a patient of anxiety disorder? What about the never-ending therapies and frequent changing of therapists? That's not the life we envisage for you at all. Therefore, prepare to fight back and reclaim your life now.

Worry can keep you restless, afraid, and helpless. If you've formed the habit of worrying all the time, you'll be susceptible to anxiety disorder. Also, you will not be a problem-solver. Instead, people will see you as an alarmist. Don't blame them because worry closes your eyes to solutions and opens them to the worst-case scenarios. Every problem needs a solution and not someone to escalate issues with fruitless worry. Therefore, if you are tired of being a worrywart, do all it takes to stop now.

Fear is another deadly enemy we dwelt on here. It can rob you of your future if you leave it. Fear can keep you stagnant static. The feeling itself is terrible, and the results are also terrifying. If you don't start facing your fears off, how are you going to be free and happy?

Already, we've shared the simple solutions to worry, anxiety, and fear. It's over to you now, to take the bull by the horn and liberate yourself from these three enemies. Close your eyes and imagine that you are moving towards your life goals. All of a sudden, a wall comes between you and your destination. What are you going to do? Turn back and start afresh? Or are you going to climb over the wall and achieve your goals? All you need to do is to follow the simple steps, exercises, and tips we've shared in this e-book. Each one can only take 10 minutes of your time and nothing more. Rome isn't built in a day. Start now and gradually find your way to living your best life with courage and confidence by making little changes, 10 minutes each day.

Bonus tip, carve out 10 minutes of your time every day as your worry & anxiety-free time. Refuse to give in to worry in these ten minutes no matter what happens. Even if the pressure comes to distract you or drag you out from this precious time, fight back, and protect your haven.

If you're thinking of what to do while enjoying your worry-free time, do something creative, think about happy moments of your life or share some love. The main thing is, don't do anything that'll lead to worry. Instead, let it be a "me time" and nothing else. Please stay away from your computer, handphones, and tablets. Turn off your handphones. Things that we'll recommend you to do in this precious 10 minutes, would be to read a novel, a comic, look out the windows, take a walk, or try out any of the activities in our last chapter.

To make it more exciting and effective, fix a particular time for this "me time" every day. If you decide on when it will be, try hard to commit to it. It may be difficult to keep to it initially, but once it becomes a habit, you'll look forward to it every day. The best part is that your friends and family will come to respect those precious ten minutes as well. If you can observe this routine every day, you'll discover that it's better to be free than to burden your heart with worry.

Remember, your life, your treasure. Take care of it.